Apprentice (

Non-Calculator Functional Maths Level 2 Worked Examples

Wilfred Wright

About this Book

This book will help you revise and pass the Functional Maths Level 2 non-calculator exam. It contains worked examples covering **the new Functional Skills curriculum**. I recommend that you use this book in this way:

- Read the question
- Try it out
- Compare your answers to mine.

As the word implies, non-calculator means that you need to be able to add, subtract, multiply and divide by hand. I have included how to do this at the start of the book. **You must learn your times table.**

Finally, work through each question in the worked example section. If you feel that you need more practice, go online and download some sample papers.

Apprentice Guides are short books aimed at giving busy apprentices and others the knowledge and skills they require to help them complete their apprenticeship successfully.

TABLE OF CONTENTS

How to answer maths exam questions

1. Read the question
2. Check how many marks
3. Highlight keywords (share, round, cover etc)
4. Conversions (check for different units, e.g. g, kg; mm, cm)
5. Work out (add, subtract, multiply, divide)
6. Check your answer (reverse calculation, rounding)
7. Check if the answer makes sense.
8. Work with small numbers as you do not have a calculator.
9. Example: convert from mm to cm etc to get a smaller number to work with.

ADDITION AND SUBTRACTION

- Line up the numbers in columns
- Write the carry number in the same place

Example: What is 2444 + 94 + 3335?

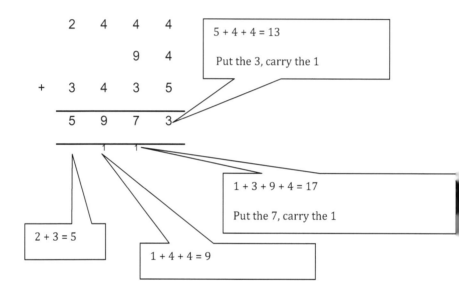

5 + 4 + 4 = 13

Put the 3, carry the 1

1 + 3 + 9 + 4 = 17

Put the 7, carry the 1

2 + 3 = 5

1 + 4 + 4 = 9

Example: What is 4125 – 837?

First we round: 4000 – 800 = 3200

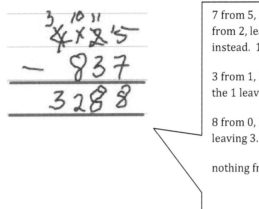

7 from 5, I cannot so I take 1 from 2, leaving 1 and getting 15 instead. 15 – 7 = 8

3 from 1, I cannot so take 1 from the 1 leaving 0. 11 –3 = 8

8 from 0, I can't so I take 1 from 4 leaving 3. 10 – 8 = 2

nothing from 3 is 3.

TIMES TABLE

- Helps with Multiplication and Division
- Pay particular attention to 6, 7 , 8 and 9 tables
- Remember that you can turn around, e.g. 7 x 6 is the same as 6 x 7
- When you multiply by an even number, you always get an even number e.g. 2 x 7 = 14
- In the 5 times table, all numbers end in 5 or 0
- In the 10 times table, all numbers end in 0
- In the 9 times table, the figures in the answers always add up to 9, 9 x 6 = 54 (5 + 4 =9)
- A number squared is a number multiplied by itself, e.g. 7 x 7 = 49 = 7^2

Table Grid

X	1	2	3	4	5	6	7	8	9	10
1	1	2	3	4	5	6	7	8	9	10
2	2	4	6	8	10	12	14	16	18	20
3	3	6	9	12	15	18	21	24	27	30
4	4	8	12	16	20	24	28	32	36	40
5	5	10	15	20	25	30	35	40	45	50
6	6	12	18	24	30	36	42	48	54	60
7	7	14	21	28	35	42	49	56	63	70
8	8	16	24	32	40	48	56	64	72	80
9	9	18	27	36	45	54	63	72	81	90
10	10	20	30	40	50	60	70	80	90	100

MULTIPLY BY 10 AND 100

- Multiply by 10, numbers move one column to the left

H	T	U	
	7	3	X 10
7	3	0	

- Multiply a whole number by 10 by adding a 0 to the end
- Multiply by 100, numbers move two columns to the left

Th	H	T	U	
		7	3	X 100
7	3	0	0	

- Multiply a whole number by 100 by adding two 00 to the end

MULTIPLY LARGE NUMBERS

Example : Calculate 234 x 75 using the traditional method:

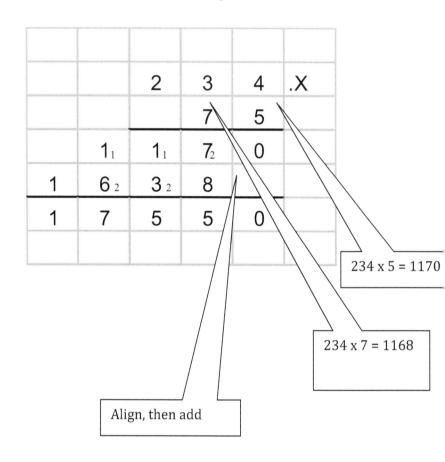

234 x 5 = 1170

234 x 7 = 1168

Align, then add

DIVIDE BY 10 AND 100

- Divide by 10, numbers move one column to the right

H	T	U	
6	8	0	÷ 10
	6	8	

- Divide by 100, numbers move two columns to the left

Th	H	T	U	
7	3	0	0	÷ 100
		7	3	

DIVIDE LARGE NUMBERS

Example: What is 646 ÷ 17? Using the traditional method

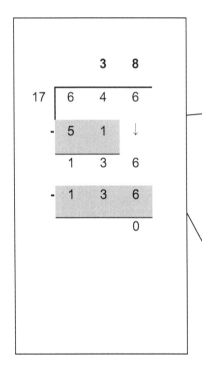

Step 1: Write down the first five numbers of the 17 times table:

1 x 17 = 17

2 x 17 = 34 (17 + 17) ; just add 17 to the first answer

3 x 17 = 51 (34 + 17) ; add 17 to the answer before

4 x 17 = 68 (51 + 17) ; and so on

5 x 17 = 85 (68 + 17)

Step 2: 64 is more than 51 but less than 68. Take the smaller, so 51 which is 3 x 17

Step 3: Write 3 at the top and 51 under the 64

Step 4: Take away 51 from 64, giving 13

Step 5: Bring the 6 down. This gives 136

Step 6: Continue the times table until we get a number larger than or equal to 136

So

6 x 17 = 102 (85 + 17)

7 x 17 = 119 (102 + 17)

8 x 17 = 136 (119 + 17) ; Bingo. We can stop here.

BODMAS

- Bodmas helps with the order in which you calculate.

B	O	D	M	A	S
Brackets	Other	Divide	Multiply	Add	Subtract

- Start with Brackets, then Other (such as squares), then Divide, followed by Multiply, then Addition and Finally Subtraction

Example: Find without using a calculator

1) 4 + 2 x 3 = 10 (multiply 2 x 3 first)

2) 16 – 8 ÷ 4 = 14 (divide 8 by 4 first)

EXAMPLE 1

Bill is a builder.
On Monday he made mortar mix.
He used 24 kg of sand and 5 kg of cement.

On Tuesday Bill will make the same type of mortar mix.
He will use 36 kg of sand.

How much cement does he need to make the same type of mortar mix?

Answer:

24 kg of sand for 5 kg of cement.

He now has 36 kg of sand.

The trick is to look at the relationship between 24 and 36. **The common number is 12: 12 x 2 = 24, 12 x 3 = 36.**

So, if Bill had 12 kg of sand, he will need 5/2 = 2.5 kg of cement.

Ratio and proportion involves multiplying and dividing.

So, for 36 kg of sand (3 x 12), he will need 2.5 x 3 kg of cement

7.5 kg.

EXAMPLE 2

a) Write 3.62927 correct to 3 decimal places.

Answer:

This is the 3 numbers after the dot. As the fourth number is 2 (less than 5), you do not round.

3.629

b) Here is a formula

$P = 3T^2$

Work out P, when T = 10

Answer:

Replace T with 10,

T^2 means T x T (2 or squared means multiply by itself)

$10^2 = 10$ x $10 = 100$

$3T^2 = 3$ x 10 x $10 = 300$

EXAMPLE 3

Lizzie buys 3 clocks for a total cost of £50 at a car boot sale.
She sells 2 of the clocks for £22 each and the other clock for
£20
Lizzie thinks she has made a profit of over 30% of the cost of
the clocks

Is Lizzie correct?
Show why you think this.

Answer:
2 clocks for £22 each, means she gets 2 x 22 = £44
Third Clock for £20, so
Lizzie gets £44 + £20 = £64

Profit = £64 - £50 = £14
Original cost = £50

30% of £50 is 30 x 50 and divide your answer by 100.

30 x 50 = 1500
1500/100 = 15

Lizzie is wrong: £14 is less than £15.

EXAMPLE 4

A car can travel 480 miles on a full tank of petrol. The tank holds 60 litres. A driver fills the tank and sets off on a journey.

How many litres of petrol will be left when the car has travelled 360 miles?

Answer:
480 miles on 60 litres.

Easier to divide by 60 to work out distance travelled on 1 lite.
1 litre = 480/60 = 8 miles.

So, how many litres used for 360 miles. This is the same as saying, how many times 8 goes into 360
360/8 = 180/4   (divide top and bottom by 2)
180/4 = 90/2 (divide top and bottom by 2)
90/2 = 45 litres.
So, we will have 60 – 45 = 15 litres left.

EXAMPLE 5

The probability that a salesperson will get an order from a visit to a customer is 1/4.

She has 2 visits tomorrow.

What is the probability that she will get orders from both visits tomorrow?

Give your answer as a fraction in its simplest form.

Answer:

Probability of getting an order from first visit = ¼

Probability of getting an order from second visit = ¼

Probability of getting an order from both visits. (You times as this is a combined event)

¼ x ¼ = 1/16

EXAMPLE 6

Usha is a local councillor.

She wants to write about a new housing development.

The diagram shows the space for the new development.

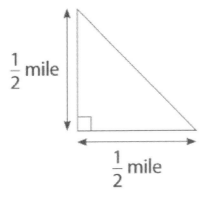

Usha thinks that the area of the development will be greater than the total area of 50 football pitches.

Usha knows

- a football pitch is rectangular 100m by 50m
- 1 mile = 1600m.

Will the area of the development be greater than the total area of 50 football pitches?

Answer:

This requires conversion. As everything is in m, convert miles to m.

1 mile = 1600 m, so ½ mile = 1600/2 = 800 m

You must also know the area of a triangle by heart!

Area of triangle = base x height / 2

Area of development = 800 x 800 /2 = 800 x 400 m².

(Leave as it is for now)

Area of rectangle = 100 x 50 m²

How many times would this go into the area of development?

So we are looking at (800 x 400) / (100 x 50).

Let's do this in two stages 800/100 = 8

400/50 = 8

So we get 8 x 8 = 64 times.

64 football pitches.

Usha is wrong.

Example 7

Alex, Jas and Stef each get a student loan to help with living expenses.

Stef's loan is for £9000

She budgets two fifths of her loan for food, and one-sixth for travel.

How much money will be left from her loan for rent and other spending?

Answer:

2/5 of 9000 for food.

Divide by the bottom first: 9000/5 = 1800.

Times your answer by the top: 1800 x 2 = 3600

1/6 of 9000 for travel.

9000/6 = 1 500

Amount for food and travel: 3600 + 1500 = 5100

Amount left = 9000 – 5100= £3900

EXAMPLE 8

Example: Work out the median of the following numbers 2, 4, 2, 3, 7.

Answer:

Median: Put the numbers in ascending order from smallest to the largest.

2   2   3   4   7

Then cross the ends off (shade off) until you are left with one number. If you are left with two, work out the mean of these two numbers.

EXAMPLE 9

Simon is redesigning his garden. He has drawn his garden on the diagram below where 1 square = 1500mm.

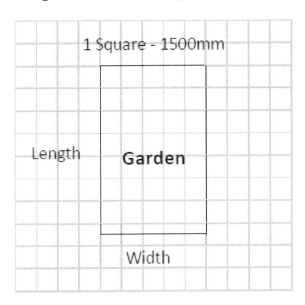

Using the grid, calculate the actual length of the garden in metres?

Answer:

The length of the garden is 7 ½ squares.

1 square = 1500 mm = 1500/10 = 150 cm = 150/100 = 1.5 m

7 x 1.5 = 10.5 m

½ a square = 1.5/2 = 0.75 m

7 ½ squares = 10.5 + 0.75 = 11.25 m

EXAMPLE 10

The distance between two villages on a map measures 6.2 centimetres.

The map has a scale 1:25 000

What is the actual distance between the two villages in kilometres?

Give your answer to 2 decimal places.

Answer:

Scale means 1 cm on the map is 25,000 cm on the ground.

Convert cm to m : Divide by 100 (**getting your numbers small**)

25,000/100 = 250 m

1000 m is 1 km

250 m = 250/1000 = ¼ m (4 x 250 = 1000)

6.2 on the map is 6.2 x ¼ m = 6.2/4 = 3.1/2 (divide top and bottom by 2)

= 1.55 km

Printed in Great Britain
by Amazon

34721241R00016